Ghost Jokes

Q: How do ghosts stay fit?

A: With routine hexorcise

Q: Have you found out about the ghost that went on an African safari with his family?

A: He was a huge game-hunter!

Q: How can a ghost style their hair?

A: With scare dryer!

Q: How do ghosts fly in between places?

A: On a scareplane!

Q: Where is the unusual ghost from?

 A: A much far-off terror-tory!

Q: Was the story concerning the lady that wished to marry a ghost true?

A: No one recognizes what she was assuming!

Q: What type of street would certainly a ghost choose?

A: A dead end!

Q: How can you inform if somebody will die?

A: He comes to be light like a sheet!

Q: What did the mother ghost tell the impolite child ghost?

A: Spook if you're startled to!

Q: How does a ghost like an egg?

A: Terrorfried!

Q: What European capital do ghosts like to visit?

A: Boodapest

Q: Why is a Ghost like an Empty House?

A: Because they don't have a body!

Q: When do ghosts play techniques with each various other?

A: April Ghoul's Day

Q: Where would you like to consume a ghost for supper.

A: Pizza Haunt!

Q: What did one ghost state?

A. I'm sorry, but individuals are not my idea!

Q: What did the ghost teacher say to her class?

A: Watch, and also I'll look at it again!

Q: What did the little ghost of a child claim to the beautiful lady ghost?

A: You are so attractive!

Q: In what layout do young ghosts finish their research?

A: Exorcise books!

Q: What occurred to the ghost when he thought of going to a celebration.

A. He was so nervous that he would certainly terrify everybody off!

Q: What did the ghost claim to the haunted house's inhabitants?

A: Halt! Exists a ghost there?

Q: What did the ghost consume for lunch today?

A: A Booloney Sandwich!

Q: Why did the ghost see the theme park

A: He desired the roller-ghoster!

Q: Which day do ghosts like?

A: Moandays

Q: What kind of songs do ghosts enjoy to dance to?

A: Soul Music!

Q: Who did the ghost invite?

A: Anyone that he might discover!

Q: What are the names of students in ghost schools?

A: Ghoulboys & ghoulgirls

Q: What instructions did the ghost offer to the goblin?

A: Make a scary turn on Scare Street

Q: What did the mommy ghost say to the youngster ghost when he went outside to play?

A: Don't obtain your sheets unclean!

Q: What do you call a ghost that is constantly asleep?

A: Lazy bones!

Q: What did the ghost consume for supper

A: Spook-ghetti!

Q: Why aren't ghosts great magicians?

A: You can see through all their techniques!

Q: What is a ghost-proof bike?

A: One without spooks!

Q: What is the preferred Wild West community of a ghost?

A: Tombstone

Q: How can you get a ghost lie level?

A: Use a level

Q: Have you become aware of the ghost that liked doing household chores?

A: He brushes up the floor with the oooover!

Q: Why are haunted homes so loud in April?

A: This is when the ghosts begin shrieking!

Q: Why were the ghosts damp as well as so worn out?

A: They had just dread-ged that lake!

Q: Which ghost had way too much gruel?

A: Ghouldilocks

Q: What sort of footwear do ghosts make use of?

A: Boots

Q: What is the preferred city of a ghost?

A: Mali Boo!

Q: What do you call a ghost who has a broken leg?

A: A goblin hoblin'!

Q: What do you call a ghost that haunts just the Town Hall?

A: The nightmayor

Q: Have you heard about the unwell ghost of old?

A: He had a horrible ooooooooooo-ping coughing!

Q: What do ghosts consume alcohol most?

A: Ghoulaid!

Q: Where do ghosts obtain mail?

A: At a ghost workplace!

Q: What do ghosts see at night?

A: Skelly vision!

Q: What's a ghost fighter?

A: A Phantom weight!

Q: When do ghosts typically appear?

A: Right prior to someone shouts!

Q: Which Central American country has the highest number of spooks in its region?

A: Ghosta Rica

Q: Which ghost are the very best professional dancers?

The Boogie Man!

Q: What occurred to a ghost who asked for a beverage in his local bar?

A The bartender stated, "Sorry. We don't serve spirits."

Q: What do you get if you cross Bambi and also a ghost with?

A: Bamboo

Q: What do ghosts drink every morning?

A: Coffee made with one scream as well as 2 sugars

Q: What did the little ghost present his mom for Mother's Day this year?

A: An arrangement of flowers

Q: What do you call a ghost inside a torn sheets?

A: A Holy Terror!

Q: How does the ghost-song-and-dance team make a living?

A: By appearing on television spooktaculars

Q: What do ghosts love about riding horses?

A: Ghoulloping

Q: What do Australian ghosts share?

A: Boo-merangs!

Q: How can a ghost begin a letter?

A: Tomb you might be concerned!

Q: Have you read about the ghost comic

A: He obtained booed off the phase!

Q: What is the favored treat of a ghost?

A: Ice yell!

Q: Where do child ghosts go in the day?

A: Day-scare!

Q: What did the daddy ghost tell the baby ghost?

A: Fasten your sheet belt!

Q: Where can a ghost fill up his vehicle with gas?

A: At an abominable station!

Q: What is the first point that ghosts do after they get in a vehicle?

A: Bookle their seat belts

Q: What kind of mistake did the ghost make

A: A Boo boo!

Monster Jokes

Q: What do they consume for lunch at a Monster School

A: Human bean, steamed legs as well as eyes-cream

Q: Why did the monster repaint his face in rainbow shades

A.He wanted a hiding location in the crayon box.

Q: What did one Frankenstein's ears tell the other?

A: We survive on the same block!

Q: What occurred to Ray after he was struck by a man-eating beast?

A.He was an ex-Ray!

Q: What was the favorite play of the beast?

A: Romeo, Ghouliet

Q: Why did the beast quit playing with its sibling?

A.He became tired by kicking him around throughout the day.

Q: What does a courteous animal state to you when he initially satisfies you?

A: Please consume me!

Q: What does a beast do if he loses his mind?

A.He asks for the head hunter!

Q: What delivers beast's children?

A: The Frankenstork

Q: How can you tell an excellent from a wicked monster?

A: If you can live with the experience, it's great!

Q: What do you call a computer mouse efficient in getting a titan?

A: Sir.

Q: What do you call a clever beast?

A: Frank Einstein!

Q: Where do area beasts live?

A: In far distant terror-tory!

Q: What is one of the most hard thing about making monster brew?

 A: Stirring It!

Q: How can you stop an impressive from scenting?

A: Cut its nose!

Q: What would certainly happen if a large, fat, and also hirsute creature placed on a red t-shirt.

A: A larger target!

QHave your heard of the five-legged monster?

A: His trousers fit him like a handwear cover!

Q: What did the beast tell his medical professional?

A: I feel awful!

Q: Where do beasts get hair done?

A: At The Ugly Parlor!

Q: What do sea monsters eat for supper?

A: Fish, and ships.

Q: What do you get when you cross a beast and also a flea?

A: Very terrified dogs!

Q: Why did Frankenstein stop boxing?

A.Because his excellent looks was essential to him!

Q: What aftershave do monsters make use of?

A: Brute.

Q: What is the distinction between a monster as well as an ape?

A: A beast produces bigger holes in wall surfaces!

Q: What happened to Frankenstein's uranium when he swallowed it?

A.He had an atomic pain!

Q: Why did the monster visit the healthcare facility?

A: To have his ghoulish-stones eliminated

Q: Where can you locate beast boogers

A: At the end of a monstrous' fingers!

Q: Have you found out about the man who sent his photo to a lonesome-.

hearts team?

A. They sent it back to state they weren't so lonely!

Q: What should you do if a person goes through your front door and also assaults you?

A: Run through the back entrance also quicker!

Q: What did the substantial, hirsute beast do after he lost his hand?

A.He went into the pre-owned store!

Q: Did you find out about the guy that shed his hair during the war?

A.He lost his hair in a hair raid.

Q: Why did the monster tear his nose off?

A. To see the factors it ran!

Q: Why was the beast standing on his heads?

A: He was reorganizing points in his head!

Q: Where is the temple of the beast?

A: On its side!

Q: What makes a perfect present for an impressive?

A: Five pairs of gloves, one for each and every hand.

Q: What does a starving monster do when he's had way too much ice cream?

A: Eat more gelato!

Q: What do you obtain when you blend a purple pastel as well as a male-eating monster?

A: A purple person eater!

Q: How can you tell if a person has a glassy eye?

A. It comes out in discussion!

Q: What is the favorite drink of a beast?

A: Demonade.

Q: What sort of monster can you put in your cleaning equipment?

A: A laundry n' put on wolf.

Q: Why did this beast drive a dead male in his cars and truck?

A.Because (carcass?) he was a car-case!

Q: Why did this monster consume a liter antifreeze?

A.So he would not need to purchase a winter layer!

Q: What can a beast do to you that you can not?

A: Count up to 25 on your fingers!

Q: Why did this beast freeze the cake?

A.Because he heard that the cake called for icing!

Q: What beast plays the most April Fools jokes A: Prankenstein!

Q: What is a monster like an jack-o'- light?

A: They both have empty heads!

Q: What is huge, furry as well as dangerous, with sixteen wheels?

A: A giant on roller-skates.

Q: What do young female beasts do at celebrations

A: They are looking for edible bachelors.

Q: What type of beast could sit on your finger? The bogeyman!

Q: What is the distinction in between a silly animal and a birthday celebration candle,?

A: The candle is much brighter!

Q: What do you get when you go across a tall, eco-friendly monster with a pen and also a pen?

A: The Ink-credible Helk!

Q: What would you call a huge, unsightly, fuzzy, slobbering monster wearing earplugs?

A: Anything that you wish to. He will not even hear you.

Q: What occurs if a massive unshaven monster beings in front you at the flicks.

A: You will not see most of the film!

Q: What occurs if a big, hirsute beast walks on Batman and Robin's feet?

A: Flatman, Ribbon!

Q: Why was the two-headed beast at the top of the school's class?

A: Because it's far better to have 2 heads than one!

Q: Why was the beast fined for Thanksgiving?

A: He surpassed the feed restriction.

Q: How does Frankenstein enter into his chair?

A: Bolt upright!

Q: What is big and unshaven?

A: A traffic congestion beast!

Q: What occurred to the perfume container that was taken by a monster?

A: He was convicted for fragrancy.

Q: If storks have human infants, then what concerning beast children?

A: Monster storks!

Q: How can a monster begin a fairy story?

A: Once upon an eel!

Q: What kind of publications did Frankenstein take pleasure in reading?

A: One on a story in a cemetery!

Q: What would you get if a beast was coupled with a Thanksgiving treat.

A: Bumpkin pie!

Q: What is the engraving on Frankenstein's tomb?

A: Here exists Frankenstein. Let him relax in peace!

Q: How did the monster recover his sore throats?

A. He invested the entire day gargoyling.

Q: Have you found out about the beast with ten arms however no legs?

A: He was all thumbs as well as fingers!

Q: How do you deal with a monstrous?

A: Very politely, from far!

Q: Why did Frankenstein smother his girlfriend to death

A: He had a crush upon her!

Q: Why did he lie on his back to the monster?

A: To trip up low-flying planes!

Q: How can you kill a monstrous?

A Throw egg at him. He will certainly be egg-terminated.

Q: How can you stop a garden monster from digging in your garden?

A: Take his shovel away!

Q: How can man-eating beasts be counted to a 100

A: On their moles!

Q: What do you do when you have an environment-friendly beast in your life?

A: Bring it to the sun till it ripens!

Q: What monster flies his kite during a storm?

A: Benjamin Frankenstein!

Q: What occurred when 2 giants jumped off a cliff with each other?

A: Boom Boom!

Q: What took place to Frankenstein while he got on the road?

A.He was stopped and also fined $100, and after that took down for 6-months!

Q: What does a monster mommy claim to her children at dinnertime?

A: Do not talk to any person in your mouth!

Vampire Jokes.

Q: What is Dracula's favored gelato taste?

A: Vein-illa!

Q: What do you obtain when you cross Dracula and also Sir Lancelot?

A: A bite of beaming shield.

Q: Why is it so difficult to compete with a vampire?

A: Because there are always blood on the ground!

Q: What type of people are vampires attracted to?

A: Type O favorable!

Q: Why was Dracula always all set to assist young vampires.

A.Because it was fun to fulfill brand-new individuals in business!

Q: What are webbed feet or fangs? A: Count Qackula!

QHave you heard about the vampire that joined an orchestra?

A.He stood up on the roof and also did lightning!

Q: What is it called when you are snagged by a vampire?

A: Necking.

Q: What is a vampire's favored drink?

A: A Bloody Mary.

Q: What do you obtain when you cross a clown entertainer as well as a vampire?

A: Something that is straight for the juggler.

Q: Why did the McDonald's vampire go insane?

A.He was thrilled by the catsup, and he intended to get a blood transfusion.

Q: Why are vampire households so close with each other?

A: Because water is thinner than blood!

Q: What does Dracula inform his sufferers?

A: It's been great gnawing at you!

Q: Where's Dracula?

A: The Vampire State Building.

Q: Why did the Vampire remain on a Pumpkin?

A: It wanted squash!

Q: What do vampires kind with A: Blood type authors!

Q: What do vampires require to get a cold?

A: Coffin syrup.

Q: Why does Dracula not have close friends?

A.Because it's a pain!

QDid Dracula wish to be a comedian?

A.He is seeking a cryptwriter!

Q: What do you get when you cross a vampire with a mommy.

A: You would not desire it unwrapped!

Q: How do you speak with a vampire best?

A: By phone and long distance.

Q: What do you obtain when you cross Dracula as well as a snail?

A: The globe's slowest vampire.

Q: Why did Dracula visit the dental professional?

A.He wanted a much better attack!

Q: Where do vampires eat their lunch?

A: At our casketeria.

Q: Why did the vampire visit the hospital?

A.He wished to eliminate his macabre stones!

Q: What did the vampire consume to remain sane?

A: Necktarines.

Q: How do vampires keep their breath fresh and great?

A: They make use of extractor fangs.

Q: Can you call a holiday committed to vampires?

A: Fangsgiving day!

Q: What is Dracula's favored treat?

A: Leeches, as well as shout!

Q: How does Dracula like his food to be served?

A: In bite-sized pieces!

Q: What does Dracula inform Dracula before he leaves for work at evening?

A: Have some fun!

Q: Why was the vampire let down with his dog?

A: It was all bark, no bite!

Q: Why did Dracula always take a trip in his coffin?

A.Because his entire life is at stake!

Q: What occurred to the vampires when they initially met?

A: It was love at first sight!

Q: How can a vampire clean his home?

A: With a target cleaner.

Q: Why would the vampire not eat his soup.

A: It was clotted!

Q: In what do vampires go across oceans?

A: Blood vessels.

Q: What is the name of a vampire that can lift autos?

A: Jacku-la!

Q: Where did the initial American vampires show up?

A: Newfang-land.

Q: What do you consider vampire films?

A: Fangtastic.

Q: How does a witch state "bye-bye!" to a vampire.

A: So long sucker!

Q: Why did Dracula miss lunch?

A.Because it had not been essential to him!

Q: How does Dracula stay fit?

A: He plays batminton!

Q: Why is the vampire considered unsuspecting?
A: Because I was a total fool!
Q: Why did the vampire determine to occupy acting?
A: It was in his blood!
QHave you read about the vampire that got wed?
A: He suggested his goul-friend!
Q: How can you join a Vampire Fan Club.
A: Send us your name, address and blood type! Q: What is Dracula's preferred animation?
A: Batman.

Q: Why did the vampire have pedestrian eyes.

A. They looked both ways prior to going across!

Q: Have you found out about the vampire that passed away from a damaged heart.

A.He loved in blood vessel!

Q: What is the preferred slogan of the vampire?
A: Please give blood!
Q: What do vampires make use of to make sandwiches?

A: Self increasing dough.

Q: How can a vampire enter his residence?

A: Through a bat flap!

Q: What is a vampire's favorite activity?

A: Ingrave-ing.

Q: What happened to the two crazy vampires,.

A. They both obtained a little insane!

QWhich Vampire attempted to eat James Bond's flesh?

A: Ghouldfinger.

Q: How are vampires pertaining to false teeth?

A: They come out at night!

QWhich Vampire consumed the gruel of 3 bears?

A: Ghouldilocks.

Q: Why was this young vampire a failing.

A.Because of the view blood, he passed out! Q: What did the courteous vampire inform you?

A: Fang thanks quite!

Q: What was Dracula's favored fruit?

A: Blood oranges.

Q: What do you get when you cross Dracula as well as Al Capone?

A: A fangster!

Q: What do vampires do at 10 on a daily basis?

A: A casket splitting!

Q: Who is the most likely vampire to fall in love?

A: The lady's door!

Q: When do vampires bite?

A: OnWincedays.

Q: Why do vampires despise disagreements.

A: Because their cross!

Q: What does a vampire stand on after taking a shower?

A: A bat mat!

Q: What did the vampire do at the blood bank?

A: He made a withdrawal!

Q: Why is Hollywood filled with vampires?

A: They require someone to play the bit parts!

Q: What is the first thing that vampires discover at school?

A: The alphabat!

Q: Why did the vampire delight in ballroom dance?

A: He could really get into the vaultz!

Q: Who plays center ahead for the vampire football group?

A: The ghoulscorer!

Q: How did the vampire obtain clean?

A: He took a blood bathroom!

Witch Jokes.

Q: What type of witch goes to the coastline?

A: A sandwitch!

Q: What would you get if you cross a witch with a popular film supervisor?

A: Steven Spellberg!

Q: What do you call a witch with poisonous substance ivy?

A: A scratchy witchy!

Q: How do you image yourself flying a broom?

A: By witchful thinking!

Q: What do you get when you cross a witch as well as a flea?

A: Very nervous pet dogs!

Q: Where do witches park their broom?

A: In the closet!

Q: What do you do if a witch is available in your front door?

A: Run out the back door!

Q: What does an Australian witch ride on?
A: A broomerang!

Q: Did you become aware of the witch who turned her buddy right into an egg?
A: She kept trying to poach her suggestions!

Q: When is it unfortunate to see a witch's black cat?
A: When you are a mouse!

Q: Why should males be careful of attractive witches?
A: Because they will certainly sweep them off their feet!

Q: How does a witch physician ask a woman to dance?
A: Voodoo like to dance with me?

Q: How does a witch begin a letter?
A: Tomb it may concern!

Q: What is the most effective way to chat with a witch?
A: By phone!

Q: What was the witch's favorite television show?
A: Lifestyles of the Witch and also Famous!

Q: What's worse than an upset witch?
A: A team of angry witches!

Q: Who went into a witches' den and came out alive?

A: The witch!

Q: What TV show has FBI agents and witches?

A: The Hex-Files!

Q: What did the witch say to the ugly toad?

A: I'd put a curse on you, but somebody beat me to it!

Q: What was the witches' motto?

A: We came, we saw, we conjured!

Q: What did the young witch say to her mother?

A: Can I have the keys to the broom tonight?

Q: Why do witches have stiff joints?

A: They get broomatism!

Q: How do you know when you are in bed with a witch?

A: She has a big W embroidered on her pajamas!

Q: Why was the student witch so bad at writing papers?

A: Because she couldn't spell properly!

Q: What has handles and flies?

A: A witch in a garbage can!

Q: How did the witch get lost?
A: Because her hat was pointing in the wrong direction!

Q: What do you call two witches who share a room?
A: Broom-mates!

Q: How did the ugly witch make money?
A: Posed for Halloween masks!

Q: What does a witch do if her broom is stolen?
A: She calls the flying squad!

Q: How come the air is so nice and fresh during Halloween?
A: There are so many witches sweeping the sky!

Q: What is the best way to stop infection from witch bites?
A: Don't bite any witches!

Q: What do you call a witch with one leg?
A: Eileen!

Q: How can you make a witch itch?
A: Take away her W!

Q: Why won't a witch wear a flat cap?

A: Because there's just no point in it!

Q: What was the witch's favorite pop group?

A: Broomski Beat!

Q: What kind of tests do student witches take?

A: Hex-aminations!

Q: Why did the witch wash her broom?

A: She wanted a clean sweep!

Q: What happens if you see twin witches?

A: You won't be able to tell which witch is which!

Q: What happened to the naughty witch at school?

A: She was ex-spelled!

Q: What was the witch's favorite school subject?

A: Spelling!

Q: How can you tell when witches are carrying a time bomb?

A: You can hear their brooms tick!

Q: Did you hear about the witch who was ashamed of her long black hair?

A: She always wore long gloves to cover it up!

Q: Did you hear about the witch that wasn't ugly but wasn't pretty?

A: She was pretty ugly!

Q: Why does a witch wear a pointed black hat?

A: To keep her head warm!

Q: What happened to the witch with an upside down nose?

A: Every time she sneezed he hat flew off!

Q: How do warty witches keep their hair in place?

A: Scare spray!

Q: What did the movie director say to the witch?

A: You have the perfect face for radio!

Q: How did the witch manage to stay in shape?

A: She got lots of hexercise!

Q: Have you heard about the good weather witch?

A: She is forecasting sunny spells!

Q: What do witches use pencil sharpeners for?

A: To keep their hats pointed!

Q: How do witches call home?
A: They use the terror-phone!

Q: Why did the witch keep turning people into Mickey Mouse?
A: She was having Disney spells!

Q: What runs in a witch's family?
A: Noses!

Q: What do you call a witch without a broom?
A: A witch-hiker!

Q: Is it good to drink witch's brew?
A: Yes because it's very newt-tricious!

Q: What goes cackle, cackle, boom?
A: A witch in a minefield!

Q: Why did the witch consult a psychic?
A: She wanted to know her horror-scope!

Q: Who won the witch's beauty pageant?
A: No one!

Q: What does a witch write at the bottom of her letters?

A: Best vicious!

Q: What do you call a witch who climbs up walls?

A: Ivy!

Q: How do witches lose weight?

A: They join weight witches!

Q: Who turned the lights off at Halloween?

A: A lights witch!

Zombie Jokes

Q: Why was the zombie fired from his job?

A: They needed someone more lively!

Q: How did the zombie accomplish all his goals?

A: He was very DEADicated!

Q: What do you get when you cross a snowman and a zombie?

A: Frostbite!

Q: When does a zombie sleep?

A: When he's dead tired!

Q: Where do zombies shop for clothes?

A: The monstore!

Q: Where's the safest place to be during a zombie invasion?

A: The LIVING room!

Q: How do zombies celebrate Halloween?

A: They paint the town dead!

Q: Where do zombies go swimming?

A: The Dead Sea!

Q: What do you get if you cross a zombie with a flea?

A: Lots of very scared dogs!

Q: What kind of dog is a zombie's favorite?

A: A blood hound!

Q: Why did the police officer give the zombie a ticket on Thanksgiving?

A: He was exceeding the feed limit!

Q: Why did the zombie go see the psychic?

A: To find out his horrorscope!

Q: Why was the zombie party so boring?

A: It was a dead event!

Q: What did the zombie eat for dinner when he was late?

A: The cold shoulder!

Q: What did the zombie say to his long lost friend?

A: I've been dying to see you!

Q: Why did the zombie go crazy?

A: He lost his mind a long time ago!

Q: What kind of candy do zombies dislike?

A: Life Savers!

Q: Why was the zombie standing on his head?

A: He was turning things over in his mind!

Q: What would you get if you crossed a plum with a man eating zombie?

A: A purple people eater!

Q: What did the zombie say before the fight?

A: Do you want a piece of me!?

Q: Why wouldn't the zombie cross the road?

A: He didn't have the guts!

Q: What is a baby zombie's favorite toy?

A: A deady bear!

Q: What kinds of streets do zombies live on?

A: Dead ends!

Q: Why did the zombie cross the road?

A: He was chasing the chicken!

Q: What was the zombie's favorite game?

A: Chase!

Q: What time do zombies wake up?
A: Ate o'clock!

Q: How do you stop a zombie from smelling?
A: Cut off his nose!

Q: What kind of vehicle did the zombie purchase?
A: A monster truck!

Q: How do zombies do well in school?
A: They eat lots of brain food!

Q: What is a zombie's favorite food?
A: Halloweenies!

Q: What do you call a dead bee?
A: A zombee!

Q: What was the zombie's favorite TV show?
A: Chomping on the Stars!

Q: What is black and white and red all over!
A: A nun being eaten by a zombie!

Q: What did the zombie say after he ate a comedian?

A: This tastes funny!

•••

What is the funniest joke?

Leave a Review!

9 798750 587773